A young man prays in the
Eid Gah Mosque in Kabul,
Afghanistan, on the first
day of Ramadan.

Fasting

Every year Muslim people all over the world celebrate Ramadan. We observe our most important holiday with fasting, prayer, and charity.

Prayer

< *These are pages of the Cairo Qur'an, which was made for the Sultan of Morocco in the 18th century.*

Charity

Ramadan is a holy time

because many years ago, during the month of Ramadan, our prophet Muhammad received the words of Allah (God). These teachings became the Qur'an, our holy book.

Ramadan is the ninth month of our year. Because of the lunar calendar we use, it can take place in spring, summer, fall, or winter.

When we see the crescent moon of the month of Ramadan, we know it is time to begin.

A crescent moon rises in Amman, Jordan, alongside the minaret of a mosque.

It is time to begin.

During Ramadan, adults
and teenagers fast. For a whole
month we do not eat or drink
anything from sunrise until
sunset. Not even a sip of water or
a piece of gum. Children don't
have to fast, but many of us try to
fast part of the time. We practice
for when we are older.

Muslims fast during Ramadan to
purify ourselves. We also fast so we
know what it feels like to be poor
and hungry all the time.

Muslims fast during Ramadan.

< *Abu Mofid Kosum reads the Qur'an to a
young friend outside a cabin he uses for
meditation in the Galilee region of Israel.*

We eat sahur.

During Ramadan, we get up very early in the morning, while it is still dark. Normally we would think of it as the middle of the night! We eat *sahur* to have energy for the day. Muslims all over the world eat different kinds of food at sahur. But we mostly eat cereal, bread, honey, jam, pancakes, eggs, cheese, tea, and juice.

> *An extended family in Basra, Iraq, enjoys sahur together.*

8

∨ *Elementary-school children in Jakarta, Indonesia, paint symbolic landscape pictures of Islam during Ramadan.*

It is hard to fast.

After sahur we wash

and say our morning prayers.
It is still dark. Sometimes we
go back to bed for a little to
rest. Then we go to school or
to work. It is hard to fast while
we go to school and play sports.
It is difficult for grown-ups to
work while they are fasting.
But we try to live life as usual
during Ramadan.

∧ *These girls in a
suburb of Sydney,
Australia, practice
their karate twice
a week, even
during Ramadan.*

11

At the end of every day,

after sunset, we eat another meal. It is called *iftar*. We love to eat with our grandparents, aunts, uncles, and cousins, if they live close by. If not, we eat with friends. We break our fast by drinking water and eating some dates. That is how Muhammad broke his fast. Then we eat delicious and healthful foods. We try not to eat too much!

∧ *A cannon goes off at sunset on Mount Noqum in Sanaa, Yemen, to signal the end of the fast for the day.*

> *Friends eat iftar together at a party in Potomac, Maryland.*

We break
our fast.

During Ramadan we read the Qur'an. Some people read it from the beginning to the end. That takes the whole month. We think about God. And we think about what Muhammad, our prophet, taught us. He taught us to believe in God, to pray, and to think of others.

We think about God.

∧ *A group of women read the Qur'an together at a mosque in Kuala Lumpur, Malaysia, during Ramadan.*

< In Sharjah, United Arab Emirates, a boy carries food for iftar provided by the Red Crescent, which feeds the needy during Ramadan.

> A boy prepares food to share for iftar at a mosque in Karachi, Pakistan.

We think of those who are hungry.

We give to the needy.

We give money to people who are poor or have suffered a tragedy. We think of those who are hungry every day, and we invite others to join us for iftar. Sometimes we invite our non-Muslim friends to join us.

∧ Men kneel in prayer on a rooftop in New Delhi, India, on a Friday evening during Ramadan.

We ask for forgiveness.

Toward the end of Ramadan

is the Night of Power. We spend extra hours in prayer. Sometimes we stay all night at the mosque.

At this time we forgive all who have hurt us. We ask for forgiveness from those we have hurt. We promise to serve God and to do good deeds. We promise to be better people.

< In Philadelphia, Pennsylvania, a man prays at a mosque on the last day of Ramadan. He is joined at the mosque by Muslims from West Africa, the Middle East, Europe, and other parts of the U.S.

It is Eid al-Fitr!

U.S. postage stamp ∧

< Women dance to celebrate the end of Ramadan and the beginning of Eid al-Fitr in Beijing, China.

> This man in Srinagar, India, hopes people will buy his beautiful cakes to celebrate Eid. The writing on the cake means Happy Eid.

We know it is the end of

Ramadan when we see a new crescent moon. That means it is a new month called *Shawwal.* And it is time to celebrate. It is Eid al-Fitr!

A boy waits his turn on a carousel at an Eid festival in Balkh, Afghanistan.

We visit family and friends.

> In Nepal, girls decorate their hands with henna in celebration of Eid al-Fitr.

∨ Women in Lahore, Pakistan, buy colorful bangle bracelets to wear on Eid.

We put on new clothes.

We visit with family and friends. We especially pay our respects to our oldest relatives. We give and receive little gifts and money. We share meals of delicious food. We even have carnivals and fairs.

After prayers, two boys hug each other outside the Jama Masjid, or Friday Mosque, in New Dehli, India.

Blessings to All!

Eid al-Fitr is a three-day festival. It is a happy, relaxed time after a solemn month. But we don't forget all we thought about during Ramadan. We remember what is important to us: God, friends, family, and the needy. We say to all we meet, *Eid Mubarak*, Happy Eid! And blessings to all!

MORE ABOUT RAMADAN

Contents

Just the Facts

WHO CELEBRATES IT: Muslims

WHAT: A solemn holiday during which Muslims fast, pray, think of Allah (God) and of Muhammad's teachings, give to the needy, and vow to become better people.

WHEN: Ramadan is the ninth month in the Islamic calendar, which is based on the moon. It can occur at any time of the year. Eid al-Fitr is the festival after Ramadan.

HOW LONG: Ramadan is a month; Eid al-Fitr is celebrated for three days.

RITUAL: Fasting from sunup to sundown.

FOOD: Dates are the traditional food with which to break the daily fast.

The Five Pillars of Islam

Muhammad taught us the five pillars of Islam, our religion. We follow the five pillars:

1

We believe in one God, and that His teachings came to us through the prophet Muhammad. This saying is very important to Islam: "There is no god but God."

2

We pray every day, five times a day when possible. When we pray we face toward Mecca, our holy city.

3

We are concerned with the needy, and we give to charity every year.

4

We fast during the month of Ramadan.

5

We try to make a pilgrimage to Mecca at least once in our lives.

The Muslim Calendar

A calendar is a way to divide time over days, weeks, months, and years. The calendar used in much of the world is called the Gregorian calendar. It is based mostly on the fact that it takes the Earth roughly 365 days to orbit the sun. Months are at the same time every year, in the same season.

The Islamic Calendar is a lunar calendar. It is based on the cycles of the moon. In the Islamic calendar, a month is a lunation—one full phase of the moon from new moon to new moon. There are 12 lunar months in the Islamic year and about 354 days. So because the lunar year is about 11 days shorter than the Earth's orbit around the sun, Ramadan and other Islamic holy days shift 11 days earlier each solar year. That's why Ramadan is at different seasons.

Here are some dates when Ramadan will start:

September 24, 2006
September 13, 2007
September 2, 2008
August 22, 2009
August 11, 2010

∧ *Dressed in fine robes and blowing horns, Muslim men in Nigeria take part in a special festival known as Sallah during Eid al-Fitr.*

Fatima's Fingers

In Tunisia, for iftar, after dates and soup, many people eat Fatima's Fingers. This delicious recipe is from Souad Tnani-Grissa.

Makes about 16 pieces.

INGREDIENTS:

2 hard boiled eggs, chopped
2 raw eggs, beaten
1/2 pound ricotta cheese (fresh if available)
1/3 cup chopped parsley
2 tablespoons grated Parmesan cheese
salt and pepper to taste
4 sheets phyllo dough (defrosted if frozen)
1/2 cup melted butter
an adult to help you

1. Make the filling: In a mixing bowl, combine boiled eggs, raw eggs, ricotta, parsley, Parmesan, and salt and pepper. Mix well.

2. Refrigerate filling for at least 30 minutes.

3. Preheat oven to 325° F.

4. Unroll one sheet of phyllo dough. Keep the others under a damp kitchen towel so they don't dry out. Brush phyllo sheet with melted butter.

5. Cut the phyllo sheet into four quarters.

6. Fold each quarter in half.

7. Place a tablespoon of the filling at the bottom of each folded quarter, leaving about one inch at each side.

8. Fold the bottom and roll up each quarter of dough. Press edges together, then brush with butter. Repeat with remaining sheets of phyllo dough.

9. Put the "fingers" on a cookie sheet. Bake them in the oven for about 30 minutes, or until golden brown. Transfer to a serving plate and enjoy.

Find Out More

BOOKS

Those with a star (*) are especially good for children.

Cook, Michael. *The Koran: A Very Short Introduction.* Oxford University Press, 2000. A good, comprehensive explanation of the Muslim holy book.

*Demi. *Muhammad.* Margaret K. McElderry Books, 2003. A well written and beautifully illustrated book about the prophet of Islam. It also includes good information about the history of Islam.

Esposito, John. *The Oxford History of Islam.* Oxford University Press, 2000. If you have the time or inclination, this beautifully illustrated volume is probably the book to read.

*Ghazi, Suhaib Hamid. *Ramadan.* Holiday House, 1996. A picture book about a boy and his family observing Ramadan. Non-Muslim readers will gain a greater understanding of what it is to be Muslim.

*Hoyt-Goldsmith, Diane. *Celebrating Ramadan.* Holiday House, 2001. The author follows a New Jersey boy and his family through Ramadan and Eid al-Fitr. The book is illustrated by photographs of the family.

The Islamic World: A.D. 600-1500. National Geographic Books, 2005. An extensive book for older children and adults about the beginnings of Islam.

WEB SITES

Ramadan is always spelled the same way, but there are different spellings for Eid al-Fitr, including Id al-Fitr and Eid ul-Fitr. You can search the Web under the different spellings.

http://islamonline.net/english/index.shtml
IslamOnline.net is a Web site put out by scholars of Islam around the world. It is a very extensive site for both Muslims and non-Muslims.

http://theeid.dgreetings.com/
A fun site for Eid greeting cards, wallpapers, etc. It also has sections on the traditions and history of Islam and Eid.

http://www.bbc.co.uk/schools/religion/islam/
A site put out by the British Broadcasting Company for children and teachers about Islam. Go also to *http://www.bbc.co.uk/schools/religion/islam/ramadan.shtml* for the specific page on Ramadan.

http://aa.usno.navy.mil/faq/docs/islamic.html
This site, put out by the U.S. Navy, explains the phases of the moon and the Islamic calendar. Also go to *http://aa.usno.navy.mil/faq/docs/moon_phases.html.*

http://moonsighting.com/
This Web site shows Muslims around the world how to figure out when the new month begins.

> In Paris, France, customers can buy their iftar meal at an outdoor café.

Glossary

Allah: The Arabic name for God.

Eid al-Fitr (EED-al-fitr): Eid means celebration in Arabic. Fitr means to break. So Eid al-Fitr symbolizes the breaking of the fast and also the breaking of bad habits.

Iftar (if-TAHR): The meal eaten after sundown during Ramadan.

Islam: The religion of Muslim people, founded by Muhammad in 622. It is a religion of one God.

Mecca: A holy city in Islam because Muhammad was born there. It is in the country of Saudi Arabia.

Muhammad (also spelled Mohammad or Muhammed): The man to whom the Qur'an was revealed. Called a prophet. He was born around 570. He became a prophet in 610 and died in 632.

Mosque: A Muslim place of worship.

Muslim: A follower of Islam.

Qur'an (also Koran, Quran)(kor-AHN): The sacred book of Islam, which contains the teachings of Allah as told to Muhammad by the angel Gabriel.

Sahur (sa-HOOR): The meal eaten before sunrise during Ramadan.

Where This Book's Photos Were Taken

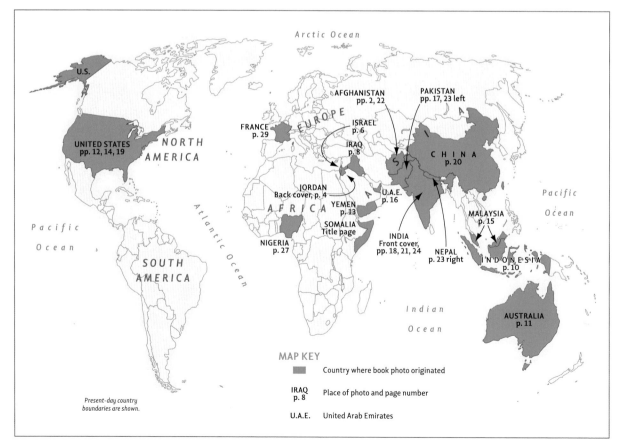

MAP KEY

Country where book photo originated

IRAQ p. 8 — Place of photo and page number

U.A.E. — United Arab Emirates

Present-day country boundaries are shown.

Ramadan: A Celebration of Faith, Family, and Community

by Dr. Neguin Yavari

The ninth month of the year in the religious calendar of Islam is called Ramadan. Ramadan is singled out as a special time because during this month God first revealed the Holy Qur'an to the Prophet Muhammad. The first verses were revealed on a night known as *Lailat al-Qadr* (the Night of Power). The exact date is not agreed upon, but the consensus is that it falls within the last ten days of the month.

Ramadan is the time of the year that provides everyone with the occasion to think more about spiritual matters, to do good work, and to spend time with and appreciate the people you love: your parents, your friends, and your neighbors. It is also a time when most adults and older children do not eat or drink throughout the day. In a direct way this fast reminds Muslims every year of the values of self-discipline and moderation. It also reminds us of the importance of generosity to others, as it makes us acutely aware of the many people in the world who have no choice but to go hungry. As we fast, we empathize with those who suffer throughout the year from the pains of hunger, malnutrition, and disease.

Not all Muslims have to fast. Islam explicitly rules against doing anything that might harm a person's own health and well-being. Therefore old people, those suffering from sickness (whether mental or physical), and pregnant women are exempt. Children also are not required to fast, because they need regular meals while they are growing.

Those who fast usually eat twice in 24 hours. One meal, called *sahur*, is taken just before sunrise, when the fast begins. The other meal, known as *iftar*, is eaten directly after sunset, when the fast ends. During the daylight hours, we do not eat any food or drink anything, including water. Iftar, the evening meal, usually lasts longer than sahur and is more substantial. It is also a time for celebration. Often extended families, including children, guests, and out-of-town visitors, share iftar together.

Ramadan is also a time of communal learning. Many Muslims devote more time to reading the Holy Qur'an in this month, either by themselves or by visiting mosques where passages are recited aloud.

The end of this month of fasting and reflection is marked by one of the most important festivals of the Islamic calendar, Eid al-Fitr (the Festival of the Breaking of the Fast). During the three days of Eid al-Fitr, everyone puts on their best clothes, and families get together or go from house to house visiting each other. Children are given small presents. Charity is particularly important on this day so that the entire community can share in the celebrations. Those people who have not been able to fast (for health or other reasons) donate sums of money, already set aside, to the poor and the needy.

The Islamic religious calendar is lunar. The months are a few days shorter than those of a solar calendar, and they are not fixed to the four seasons. The month of Ramadan, therefore, like all the other lunar months, moves through the seasons. It can occur in winter, when the days are short, or in the middle of summer, when the days are long and one has to fast for considerably longer hours. These seasonal changes and shifting hours are a reminder to Muslims to bear in mind the ever-changing nature of everyday life, while remaining steadfast to their innermost spiritual beliefs and convictions.

Neguin Yavari is Assistant Professor of Islam in the Department of Religion at Columbia University in New York.

For Nancy Sandberg, who brings the world to her fourth graders.

PICTURE CREDITS

Page 1: © Liba Taylor/Corbis; Page 2: © Paula Bronstein/Getty Images; Page 3: © Corbis; Page 4-5: © Reuters/Corbis; Page 6: © Annie Griffiths Belt/National Geographic Society; Page 8-9: © Atef Hassan/Reuters/Corbis; Page 10: © Choo Youn-Kong/AFP/Getty Images; Page 11: © Kate Geraghty; Page 12, 14: © Omar Mullick; Page 13: © Khaled Abdullah/Reuters/Corbis; Page 15: © Reuters/Corbis; Page 16: © Jorge Ferrari/epa/Corbis; Page 17: © Aamir Qureshi/AFP/Getty Images; Page 18: © David Guttenfelder/Associated Press; Page 19: © E. A. Kennedy III/The Image Works; Page 20 (top): © Associated Press; Page 20 (bottom): © Corbis; Page 21: © Sajjad Hussain/AFP/Getty Images; Page 22: © Tomas Munita/Associated Press; Page 23 (left): © Arif All/AFP/Getty Images; Page 23 (right): © Narendra Shrestha/epa/Corbis; Page 24-25: © Ami Vitale; Page 27: © Carol Beckwith & Angela Fisher/HAGA/The Image Works; Page 28: © R.B. Grissa; Page 29: © Simon Isabelle/SIPA Press; Front cover: © Gautam Narang; Back cover: © Chris Hondros/Getty Images; Spine: © Associated Press

Text copyright © 2006 Deborah Heiligman

Library of Congress Cataloging-in-Publication Data

Heiligman, Deborah.
Celebrate Ramadan & Eid al-fitr / Deborah Heiligman ; consultant, Neguin Yavari.
    p. cm.— (Holidays around the world)
ISBN 0-7922-5926-2 (hardcover)
ISBN 0-7922-5927-0 (library binding)
1. Ramadan — Juvenile literature. 2. 'Id al-Fitr — Juvenile literature. 3.   Fasts and feasts — Islam — Juvenile literature. 4.   Islam — Rituals — Juvenile literature. I. Yavari, Neguin. II. Title. III. Title: Celebrate Ramadan and Eid al-fitr. IV. Series: Holidays around the world (National Geographic Society (U.S.)).

BP186.4.H45 2006
297.3'62 — dc22

                                    2006008889

ISBN-10: 0-7922-5926-2 (trade)
ISBN-13: 978-0-7922-5926-8 (trade)
ISBN-10: 0-7922-5927-0 (library)
ISBN-13: 978-0-7922-5927-5 (library)

Book design is by 3+Co.
The body text in the book is set in Mrs. Eaves.
The display text is Lisboa.

Front cover: At a school devoted to religious studies in New Delhi, India, a boy in traditional Muslim dress reads the Qur'an.
Back cover: Girls in Amman, Jordan, celebrate Eid al-Fitr on a playground.
Title page: A young schoolgirl in Somalia studies verses of the Qur'an written on a wooden tablet called a *lawh*.

STAFF FOR THIS BOOK

Nancy Laties Feresten, *Vice President, Editor-in-Chief of Children's Books*
Sue Macy, Marfé Ferguson Delano, *Project Editors*
Jim Hiscott, *Art Director*
Lori Epstein, *Illustrations Editor*
Carl Mehler, *Director of Maps*
Priyanka Lamichhane, *Editorial Assistant*
Rebecca Hinds, *Managing Editor*
R. Gary Colbert, *Production Director*
Lewis R. Bassford, *Production Manager*
Vincent P. Ryan, Maryclare Tracy, *Manufacturing Managers*

ACKNOWLEDGMENTS

Many thanks to Karen Slattery and Raouf Grissa of Paganini Café in Doylestown, PA, for their family recipe of Fatima's Fingers, and to R.B. Grissa for taking the photo. Thanks to Hala Alkayyali for talking with me about Ramadan and Eid, and for making me feel so welcome at her Ramadan program at the Children's Museum of Manhattan. Thanks to Amel Ziad for her helpful input on the book. Thanks to the good people at the Bank Street Bookstore for leading me to the right books. Thanks to Sue Macy, who shepherded this book from the beginning almost to the end, and to Marfé Delano, who jumped right in at the end. A special thanks to Lori Epstein, for working so hard, and making miracles happen.